ORIGIN AND HISTORY

Dachshund is pronounced doxhoont (oo as in foot). In German, *dachs* means badger; *hund* means dog; *Dachshund* thus means "badger dog" in the same way we say "bird dog" or "rabbit dog." Affectionate German diminutives include "Dackel" and "Teckel."

Few breeds escape from partisan rivalry dating back to remote antiquity—although all breeds share the same derivation from common prehistoric canine prototypes—with no valid evidence tracing any continuity from far-fetched forebears, fostered by folklore or fantasy. Claims of Egyptian origin for Dachshunds, based on carvings (from about 1500 B.C.) of short-legged dogs (one with a hieroglyphic name translated as "Tekal") ignore the

Short-legged dogs like this handsome wirehaired Dachshund can be seen in ancient Egyptian hieroglyphics. Whether they are actual Dachshunds has never been proven.

fact that there were no badgers in Egypt—so no "badger" dog. Nor do they trace linguistic or biological connections with a dog developed to hunt badgers and so named in Germany at least 3,000 years and 1,000 dog generations later. Daniel's interpretation of the Old Testament handwriting on the wall (*Mene, Mene, Tekel, Upharsin*) defines Tekel as "weighed in the balances and found wanting"—an apt epitaph on illusory ancient origin!

Earliest records now available of *dogs* hunting *badgers* include several woodcuts in a book first published in 1560. These dogs had long bodies, short legs, medium-length heads, pendent ears, short necks, and sickle tails. It is noteworthy that there are smooth coats and suggestions of longhaired coats in

Early Dachshunds registered by the American Kennel Club show how little the dogs have changed in recent years. In general the dogs seem lighter than what we are accustomed to seeing today.

the longer furnishings on ears, culottes, and tails of some of the dogs illustrated.

The name "Dachshund" has been traced back to a book in German and Latin in 1681, and there are paintings dating from 1735 of unmistakable Dachshunds, identified by name as such.

Schlupfer Euskirchen. Original photograph courtesy of Major Emil Ilgner.

GERMAN HISTORY

The real origin of the Dachshund breed is embraced in the 300 years (1550-1850) during which the German forester-gamekeepers and sportsmen among the land-owning gentry— at first selecting dogs for their success in hunting badgers underground—gradually produced a badger dog better adapted by structure and temperament to cope with the dangerous claws and fangs of this formidable 25 to 40 pound antagonist. Girth of chest determines the size of burrow a Dachshund can penetrate and, therefore, the size of the adversary in residence. Always facing the possibility of a death struggle underground, where no human help could avail, a Dachshund's self-reliant use of its own armament of jaws and teeth must settle the question of survival. A Dachshund head and neck, inadequate to balance its body, would be no match for the defending opponent, any more than a small-caliber weapon is effective against large-caliber game. Within depth and height limits of the bore of the average badger tunnel, successive Dachshund generations converged more and more toward a pattern— balancing punishing head with

Schlupfer Euskirchen used in an early illustration of "perfect conformation."

Junker Schnapphahn bred by W. Falkenberg and owned by Emil Ilgner.

length of neck and body and "retractable" running gear, and combining maximum combat capacity with maximum maneuverability. Male and female Dachshunds were used interchangeably for hunting—there was no distinction of warrior armed for battle and delicately proportioned

Hundesport Waldmann bred by R. Stech and owned by Ernst von Otto-Kreckwitz.

chatelaine pursuing cultural arts at home. In addition, left to her own devices, a mother Dachshund would be responsible for bringing home the game to feed her litter. Among Dachshunds, there is no excuse for a "weaker sex," no feminine discount for head and neck equally needed for defense and offense by both sexes.

There were many other forms of game in German forests besides badgers; and because of their versatility, Dachshunds were encouraged to seek out small game on the surface and, on a five-meter leash to trail wounded game including large deer, to dispatch them and recover the venison. In packs, they also were employed successfully against wild boar. However, as their name emphasizes, their structure was specialized for pursuing appropriate game underground. By the time of the earliest preserved breeding records—about a century ago—Dachshund type, as we distinguish it today from other breeds, had become clearly defined and established. Since then, this type has been continuously improved, and the ratio of good Dachshunds has been constantly increased by selective breeding.

AMERICAN HISTORY

Earliest American records show Dachshunds first imported to the United States

This black and tan smooth Dachshund is considered one of the pillars of the breed. Although his breeder and parentage are unknown, he was owned by Freiherr von Knigge.

Sieger Elfchen vom Ammersee was born in 1935; a red smooth bitch owned by Erich Assmann and bred by Fritz Matthaey.

between 1879 and 1885; eleven Dachshunds appear in Volume II of the Stud Book of the American Kennel Club, published the latter year. Most imports have come from Germany, the country of origin; others have come from Austria, Holland, Sweden, and England.

Until after World War I, most of the comparatively few Dachshunds in this country belonged to people from Germany or with German contacts. During that war, Dachshunds—considering their built-in resistance to regimentation—were very unfairly used as cartoon symbols to rally anti-German sentiment, and the breed received a severe setback. A very long time ago, when we walked our Dachshunds every day in New York City, we were challenged by unfriendly comments of "Frankfurter dogs" and "German sausage dogs." To admire Dachshunds was regarded as much of an acquired taste as smoked oysters or Greek olives.

The Dachshund Club of America carried on a successful "educational" public relations campaign during World War II, particularly directed to newspaper and magazine editors and cartoonists, reminding them that most of the human population of this country is descended from "imported" ancestry; that the few imported Dachshunds have been "naturalized" by re-registration with the A.K.C. (American Kennel Club); that Dachshunds born here—never less than ninety nine percent of the breed—are as much

Modi vom Isartal, also born in 1935, was a black and tan dog bred and owned by Herbert Sanborn.

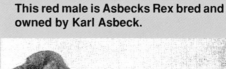

This red male is Asbecks Rex bred and owned by Karl Asbeck.

entitled to be considered American as any other American-born population. The standing of the breed, as reflected in registrations and in dog show participation, was well sustained through these hostilities, and now Dachshunds are accepted as completely as any breed.

FUNCTIONAL DESIGN

Badger earths were not air-conditioned. As oxygen was reduced by repeated breathing, it became necessary to breathe a larger volume of the depleted air to support maximum exertion. Lungs extend back as far as the soft ribs, which help the diaphragm act as bellows; the oval cross-section of the chest provides liberal room for lungs and heart without extending the shoulder structure to excessive width. The longer the rib cage, the more air could be processed, and a long rib cage also helps support the long back, resembling in design box girders.

To move this long body freely through badger burrows, it was necessary for the legs to fold to a minimum length. Anyone experimenting with a carpenter's rule can convince himself that three sections of equal length can fold shorter and extend longer than any comparable sections of unequal lengths. In the forequarters, the shoulder blade, upper arm, and forearm (elbow to wrist) do this folding. In the hindquarters, the thigh and shin bones and the "bone" from hock joint to foot are so folded in crawling through a burrow or under a bureau. Fully extended at a gallop, these same short Dachshund legs can cover an unexpected amount of ground.

When wild animals digging their tunnels encountered a rock or a large root, they dug around or over it, leaving a constriction. If an eager Dachshund forced its chest past such an obstruction and had to back up to get clear, it became important that the breastbone of the after-chest have the same gradual sled-runner up-curve as the forechest, like a shoehorn, to ease the chest over the obstruction in either direction. A cut-up (chicken-breasted) after-chest could be "hung" over such an obstacle as though by an anchor fluke. A properly

Dachshunds thrive as outdoor dogs, as they were derived to go to ground after badgers, and do best when given lots of time outside.

constructed Dachshund, with forelegs at the deepest point of the hammock-shaped keel, can crawl through a tunnel which just clears its depth from keel to withers, equally able to move its legs ahead or back. Turned-out "digging" front feet (once said to "throw dirt to the sides" where there is no room for it in a tunnel) have been replaced by snug arched feet with forward

capacity of molars. Eyes are protected by a deep setting and a well-developed surrounding bone structure. Ears set on high and well back can be drawn up over the neck out of harm's way, like small braided pigtails. A neck of good length serves the thrusting and parrying purposes of a fencer's nimble wrist. Even a tail of good size and length, in continuation of the spine, has

The longhaired variety of the Dachshund has a coat that resembles that of a setter. It is silky and long, but never exaggerated.

alignment. Too heavy a chest or too coarse bone is as much of a handicap as underdevelopment. A properly proportioned Dachshund suggests the symmetrical build and lithe agility of the middle-weight boxing champion.

A long head provides suitable accommodation for keen scenting ability and for strong jaws and teeth of maximum effectiveness, with scissor fit of incisors, interlocking fangs, and shearing

Pincers teeth, according to Engelmann.

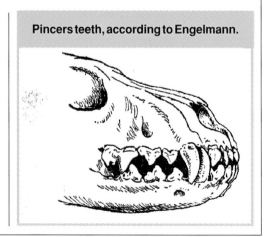

been used by a hunter's long arm forcibly to rescue many a Dachshund from places of great tightness.

A Dachshund whose skin was elastic enough to stretch and slip like a loose glove had an advantage for working in constricted space. But as soon as released, the skin should snap back to a slick fit, like the modern wrinkled socks, also is undesirable.

To avoid fatigue, straight legs with parallel gait like locomotive side-rods make efficient use of muscular energy. Viewed from the side, front, and hind leg action suggesting a broad capital "A" expends this energy on desirable reach and thrust, walking or trotting with surprising,

The dappled coloration in the Dachshund is the result of an albino variant. Very few breeds besides Dachshunds have this coloration. The Dunker of Norway and the Catahoula Leopard Dog, two very rare breeds, also come in dapple!

two-way stretch foundation garment, for a wrinkle of loose skin, by folding over, could (like a clutch) grip a dog in tight quarters. Loose skin around the head and throat could be grasped or torn by an adversary, resulting in dangerous loss of blood; skin hanging around the ankles, like apparently effortless speed and split-second rocket-like "low gear" getaway. The ninety-degree upper-arm to shoulder-blade angulation (each forty-five degrees from the vertical) provides "shock absorber" action, running or jumping. A fair clearance under the breastbone is needed, as under an automobile crankcase, to clear rough ground or the treads of a staircase. Pawing the air, like the goosestep, under chin or belly, or throwing feet in or out waste energy and are undesirable. So are "dancing" or "weaving" gaits, short stilted steps, or too many other variations from the correct gait. The back should stay level in motion; it should not roach, sag, or bounce.

Long coats are moderately furnished on the head, chest, feet and tail.

COATS AND SIZES

Two kinds of coats were developed early: the *smooth* and the *longhaired*. During the nineteenth century, to protect from briar and bramble, a third variety, with a harsh, wiry, terrier-type coat, with water-repellent undercoat, was developed— the *wirehaired*. The badger-hunting weight of thirty to forty pounds was reduced for fox to sixteen to twenty pounds; and since the turn of the century, for smaller vermin and cottontail rabbits, *miniature Dachshunds* of all three coats have been bred down as small as six and five pounds and are increasingly popular as pets.

COLORS

The original color of the Dachshund was brown, now officialy called "red." However, when a hunter with a shotgun was nervously waiting for a

The ever-adventurous Rascal, owned by Kathy Bontz, shows the Dachshund's great love of the outdoors. Rascal's thick, longhaired coat protects him from the snow and cold.

Black and tan longhaired Dachshund sitting pretty. Many would argue that the longhaired variety is the most obedient of the three, citing the breed's connection to the setter which is known for its high trainability.

The red Dachshund is among the most popular. Though some dogs look more brown than red, a good bright red is desirable.

quick brown fox to jump out of a burrow, chased by an equally thick and equally brown Dachshund, and the Dachsund beat the fox to the exit, you can guess what sometimes happened to the Dachshund! So, black and tan Dachshunds were developed by crossing to a small Bloodhound of that color, and occasional albino variants (dapples) have been highly prized as particularly suitable for trigger happy hunters. Other albino variants with tan markings include chocolate and a mousy gray (called "blue").

INTANGIBLES

Two intangible products of the formative centuries of the Dachshund also endure: the Dachshund bark, able to

Mousy gray or blue is an unusual color variation in the Dachshund, which this wirehaired dog handsomely portrays.

Tan markings can occur on any two-colored Dachshund, usually on the muzzle and over the eyes.

working hours and activities also shared their homes and many of their relaxations. Their unusual proportions lent them to a whole miscellany of sympathetically humorous illustrations and anecdotes— relating the Dachshund to the enjoyment of beer, sausages, soft living, and convival song— in which the native shrewdness of the Dachshund usually achieved its individualistic objectives. These attributes have become so much more widely known than their specialized hunting functions that outside of the German forests they more nearly represent the basis of the almost universal appeal of the Dachshunds today.

penetrate from burrow depths to the surface, and a uniquely self-reliant character developed in this one sporting breed, to engage its quarry in pursuit or mortal combat remotely underground, without guidance or support of a hunter. Dachshunds unable to rely upon themselves in the dark depths of the earth to come up with answers that worked just didn't come up at all to perpetuate their indecisions. Small wonder that today they don't turn to people much for advice.

All black and tan Dachshunds have tan markings in the same specified locations.

It is unlikely that

Single-colored Dachshunds such as this red should not have darker or lighter shaded hairs in their coats.

All in all, the Dachsunds that shared the forester's

Despite the fact that the Dachshund's long, low-slung body has its origins in utility, his appearance today is one of elegance and regalness.

you will ever want your Dachshund pet to hunt underground. But the powerful, smooth lines of the underslung Dachshund chassis represent the evolution of a design just as functional as the most modern streamlined sports cars. Your understanding of how and why the Dachshund "got that way" will better enable you to appreciate its dynamic, elegant appearance.

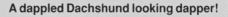
A dappled Dachshund looking dapper!

EXERCISE AND ENVIRONMENT

COLD OR HOT

Even in zero-degree weather, a Dachshund does not need a sweater or jacket outdoors, so long as it is exercising actively. If it is to stand around in frossty weather, cold wind, on wet ground, or ride in a drafty car, a garment is advisable. This may be any of several types of sweaters or coats. Be careful that it is not too tight. In *hot weather,* provide quarters that are shady, but not damp; keep fresh drinking water available, and limit exercise to the cooler early or late hours.

EXERCISE

After a puppy's frame is grown, from six months on, its muscular development depends upon the extent and nature of the exercise it gets. Each owner becomes a sculptor working constructively in the medium of living tissue. Steady, consistent walking on leash builds up proper propulsion muscles in shoulders, back, and hindquarters to bring a Dachshund to its most perfect conformation. This appearance cannot be produced by irregular romping. Walking up to two miles

The best Dachshund breeders achieve consistency and soundness with every litter, as this lovely litter of smooths bred by Kaye Ladd illustrates.

in the sun, or where the sun may strike before you return, don't leave your Dachshund—it may be overcome by the heat. Even in certain shade, be sure that windows are opened at the top. The first time you take a puppy riding in a car, also take a newspaper, in case there is any carsickness. Until you are sure of its behavior, don't feed shortly before a car trip.

FENCING AND CAGING

Partition the puppy's quarters from other rooms temporarily by using vertically sliding panels in doorways, in place of the folding lattice for children. A piece of one-eigth-inch Masonite as wide as a doorway and about twenty-four inches high can be held in place by two strips of quarter round fastened to the sides of the doorway by such thin nails that when ultimately removed no scar will show. Such a panel can be lifted out at any time you want to remove it, can be stepped over by people, leaving the door "open" for their use. When a Dachshund cannot see through this opaque barrier, it won't be tempted to make a bad habit of standing up

An exercise pen is a handy tool for confining Dachshunds at a dog show or on the road. It, of course, is not appropriate for a permanent accommodation.

Dachshunds kept outdoors require adequate fencing, unless you live in the country where there are no roadways.

against it and, thereby, over-develop its hindlegs to be taller than its shoulders or develop a concave backline. A fence, where a Dachshund makes a habit of standing up on its hindlegs, can have a horizontal opaque sheet-metal panel attached to the wire so that the Dachshund, standing on all four feet, can see under the panel without crouching yet cannot see over it by standing up against it. For adults, make it from sixteen to thirty inches; for younger or smaller Dachshunds, start with the panel lower and move it up as needed. Sitting up on its haunches does a Dachshund no harm and is a good trick.

Crates especially designed for dogs will keep a puppy confined, when desired, to a small, safe space, movable around the house, in a car, or at a dog show. If occupied regularly, a fiber carton six inches deep, inside the crate, provides a floor and draft-proof walls. In houses with areas not separated by walls or doors, the crate will prove ideal.

Fencing with Dachshunds can be tricky. Be sure that the dogs cannot *dig* underneath the structure. Remember Dachshunds were born to dig!

Regardless of the coat type of your Dachshund, grooming demands will never be exorbitant. The longhaired Dachshund's coat is easy to comb through and to keep clean and mat-free.

GROOMING

COATS

When a Dachshund's skin and diet are right, it generates its own hair oil and rubbing or brushing brings the coat to a beautiful gloss. A smooth Dachsund coat requires no more care than to stroke it vigorously with the palm of your hand, or a "hound glove," if you prefer. Longhairs and wirehairs should be brushed daily to ensure that no dead hair accumulates. Burrs or tangles should be combed out as gently as you would treat your own hair; cut them out if need be rather than pull them out.

The growth rate of the coats of many longhairs is enough to compensate for the wear of regular work in punishing thicket and thorn. Such a coat grows in such bushy profusion that vigorous combing must replace the natural wear or the dog's proper elegant outline and proportions are masked by "wool." Longer hair is specified as "fringe" or "frill" under neck and body, "feather" on ears an d behind legs, and "flag" under the tail. Excess hair should be removed from the elbows and from the feet.

A proper close harsh wirehaired coat requires no special attention, except to remove untidy hairs, particularly on feet and elbows. Less harsh coats are sometimes improved by stripping the outer coat—and plucking, or with a stripping tool, but not clippers—and vigorous daily brushing during the couple of months it takes the new coat to grow in. Professional advice and instructions are desirable. Any scissors used around the dog should have blunt points.

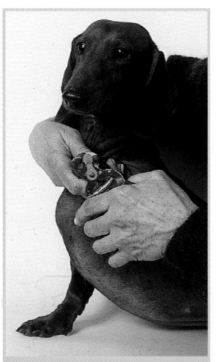

If you accustom your Dachshund to having his nails clipped at an early age, you will have a well-behaved adult to work with in the future.

BATHING

Bathing a Dachshund regularly is not necessary or desirable. A dog's body temperature is not regulated by perspiration on the skin, but is "air conditioned" by oral evaporation intensified by panting. Many a Dachshund has

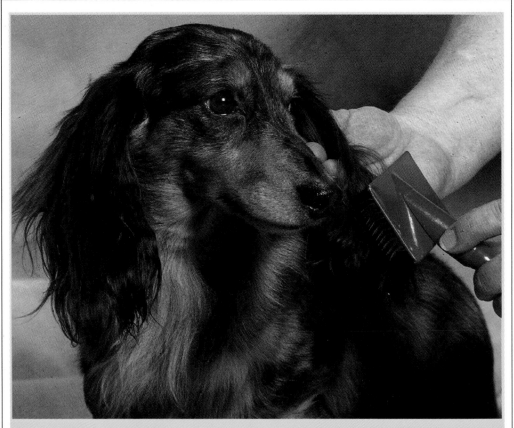

A slicker brush is handy on the longhaired Dachshund. Grooming can be a special time for the Dachshund and his favorite person—you.

The wirehaired Dachshund requires some special care to groom to perfection. His coat is more like a terrier's and needs stripping and conditioning.

lived a long, happy and socially acceptable life without one bath. Bathing robs the skin of its natural hair oil. If a dog gets into something messy or smelly, use tepid water and shampoo made especially for dogs; protect eyes and ears; lather and rinse twice until the coat is so soap-free that it "squeaks" when you rub it with your hand; towel briskly, and protect from drafts until thoroughly dry. Grooming the next day will restore natural gloss. When a Dachshund comes in from walking in wet or muddy weather, dry and clean him at the door, with a towel kept handy for that purpose.

Pet shops sell a variety of wonderful brushes. The Zoom Groom removes loose hair and dirt, stimulates the coat, and acts as a massager. Ideal for all coat types. Photograph courtesy of The Kong Company.

A grooming kit available from a pet supply shop may be the most economical way to purchase all you need to groom the Dachshund. Photograph courtesy of Wahl Clipper.

Miniature Dachshunds rarely need baths, but when they do they are cooperative and patient. Be sure to use a shampoo designed especially for dogs.

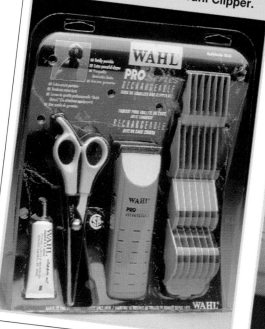

STANDARD FOR THE DACHSHUND

General Appearance—Low to ground, long in body and short of leg with robust muscular development, the skin is elastic and pliable without excessive wrinkling. Appearing neither crippled, awkward, nor cramped in his capacity for movement, the Dachshund is well-balanced with bold and confident head carriage and intelligent, alert facial expression. His hunting spirit, considered a fault.

Size, Proportion, Substance—Bred and shown in two sizes, standard and miniature, miniatures are not a separate classification but compete in a class division for "11 pounds and under at 12 months of age and older." Weight of the standard size is usually between 16 and 32 pounds.

Head—Viewed from above or from

The Dachshund is well-balanced and self-confident; he holds his head in an appropriately bold manner. This is Ch. Boondox Chaps L., owned by Dr. Roger and Deborah Brum and Sherry Snyder, a Westminster Best of Breed winner.

good nose, loud tongue and distinctive build make him well-suited for below ground work and for beating the bush. His keen nose gives him an advantage over most other breeds for trailing.

Note: Inasmuch as the Dachshund is a hunting dog, scars from honorable wounds shall not be

the side, the head tapers uniformly to the tip of the nose. The *eyes* are of medium size, almond shaped and dark rimmed, with an energetic, pleasant expression; not piercing; very dark in color. The bridge bones over the eyes are strongly prominent. Wall eyes, except in the case of dappled dogs, are a

The Dachshund's head is described as conical, as these different views show. DRAWINGS BY JOHN R. QUINN.

Keel is defined by the American Kennel Club as the rounded outline of the lower chest, between the prosternum, the posterior portion, and the sternum (breastbone).

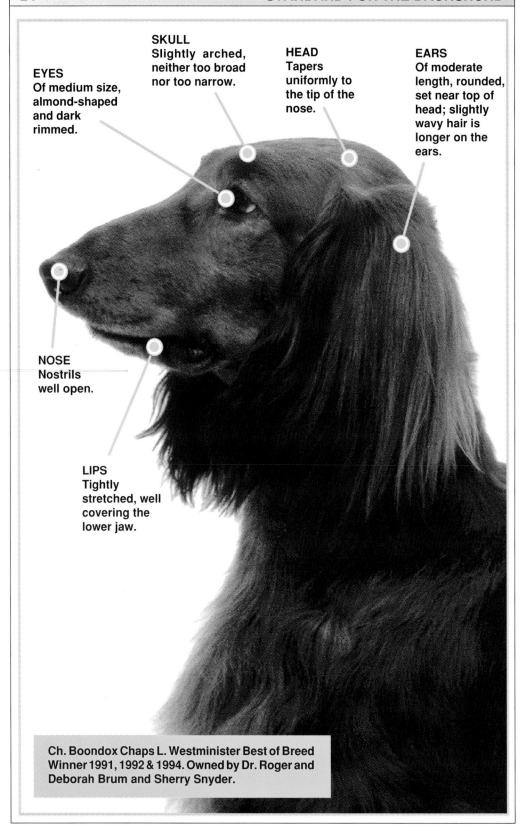

EYES
Of medium size,
almond-shaped
and dark
rimmed.

SKULL
Slightly arched,
neither too broad
nor too narrow.

HEAD
Tapers
uniformly to
the tip of the
nose.

EARS
Of moderate
length, rounded,
set near top of
head; slightly
wavy hair is
longer on the
ears.

NOSE
Nostrils
well open.

LIPS
Tightly
stretched, well
covering the
lower jaw.

Ch. Boondox Chaps L. Westminister Best of Breed
Winner 1991, 1992 & 1994. Owned by Dr. Roger and
Deborah Brum and Sherry Snyder.

serious fault. The **ears** are set near the top of the head, not too far forward, of moderate length, rounded, not narrow, pointed or folded. Their carriage, when animated, is with the forward edge just touching the cheek so that the ears frame the face. The **skull** is slightly arched, neither too broad nor too narrow, and slopes gradually with little perceptible stop into the finely-formed, slightly arched muzzle. Black is the preferred color of the nose. **Lips** are tightly stretched, well covering the lower jaw. Nostrils will open. Jaws opening wide and hinged well back of the eyes, with strongly developed bones and teeth. **Teeth**—Powerful canine teeth: teeth fit closely together in a scissors bite. An even bite is a minor fault. Any other deviation is a serious fault.

Neck—Long, muscular, clean-cut, without dewlap, slightly arched in the nape, flowing gracefully into the shoulders.

Trunk—The trunk is long and fully muscled. When viewed in profile, the back lies in the straightest possible line between the withers and the short, very slightly arched loin. A body that hangs loosely between the shoulders is a serious fault. **Abdomen**—Slightly drawn up.

Forequarters—For effective underground work, the front must be strong, deep, long and cleanly muscled. Forequarters in detail: **Chest**—The breastbone is strongly prominent in front so that on either side a depression or dimple appears. When viewed from the front, the thorax appears oval and

The wirehaired Dachshund is furnished on the jaw, eyebrows and ears with longer hair than his tight, hard body coat. The longhaired Dachshund has longer hair on the ears, but the face is free of any furnishings.

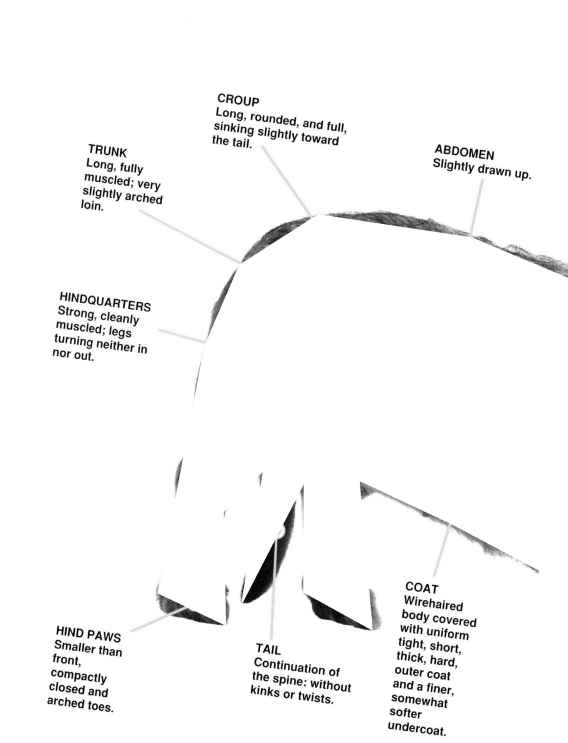

CROUP
Long, rounded, and full, sinking slightly toward the tail.

TRUNK
Long, fully muscled; very slightly arched loin.

ABDOMEN
Slightly drawn up.

HINDQUARTERS
Strong, cleanly muscled; legs turning neither in nor out.

HIND PAWS
Smaller than front, compactly closed and arched toes.

TAIL
Continuation of the spine: without kinks or twists.

COAT
Wirehaired body covered with uniform tight, short, thick, hard, outer coat and a finer, somewhat softer undercoat.

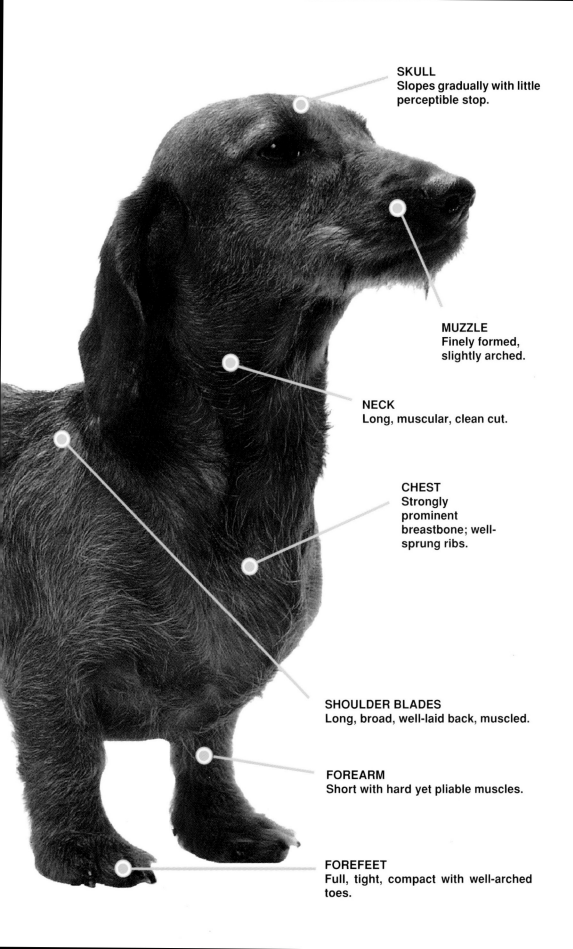

SKULL
Slopes gradually with little perceptible stop.

MUZZLE
Finely formed, slightly arched.

NECK
Long, muscular, clean cut.

CHEST
Strongly prominent breastbone; well-sprung ribs.

SHOULDER BLADES
Long, broad, well-laid back, muscled.

FOREARM
Short with hard yet pliable muscles.

FOREFEET
Full, tight, compact with well-arched toes.

extends downward to the mid-point of the forearm. The enclosing structure of well-sprung ribs appears full and oval to allow, by its ample capacity, complete development of the heart and lungs. The keel merges gradually into the line of the abdomen and extends well beyond the front legs. Viewed in profile, the lowest point of the breast line is covered by the front leg. *Shoulder Blades*—Long, broad, well-laid back and firmly placed upon the fully developed thorax, closely fitted at the withers, furnished with hard yet pliable muscles. *Upper Arms*—Ideally the same length as the shoulder blade and at right angles to the latter, strong of bone and hard of muscle, lying close to the ribs, with elbows close to the body, yet capable of free movement. *Forearm*—Short; supplied with hard yet pliable muscles on the front and outside, with tightly stretched tendons on the inside and at the back, slightly curved inwards. The joints between the forearms and the feet (wrists) are closer together than the shoulder joints, so that the front does not appear absolutely straight. Knuckling over is a disqualifying fault. *Feet*—Front paws are full, tight, compact, with well-arched toes and tough, thick pads. They may be equally inclined a trifle outward. There are five toes, four in use, close together with a pronounced arch and strong, short nails. Front dewclaws may be removed.

Hindquarters—Strong and cleanly muscled. The pelvis, the thigh, the second thigh, and the metatarsus are ideally the same length and form a series of right angles. From the rear, the thighs are strong and powerful. The legs turn neither in nor out. *Metatarsus*—Short and strong, perpendicular to the second thigh bone. When viewed from behind, they are upright and parallel. *Hind Paws*—Smaller than the front paws with four compactly closed and arched toes with tough, thick pads. The entire foot points straight ahead and is balanced equally on the ball and not merely on the toes. Rear dewclaws should be removed. *Croup*—Long, rounded and full, sinking slightly toward the tail. *Tail*—Set in continuation of the spine, extending without kinks, twists, or pronounced curvature, and not carried too gaily.

Gait—Fluid and smooth. Forelegs reach well forward, without much lift, in unison with the driving action of the hind legs. The correct shoulder assembly and well fitted elbows allow the long, free stride in front. Viewed from the front, the legs do not move in exact parallel planes, but incline slightly inward to compensate for shortness of leg and width of chest. Hind legs drive on a line with the forelegs, with hocks (metatarsus) turning neither in nor out. The propulsion of the hind leg depends on the dog's ability to carry the hind leg to complete extension. Viewed in profile, the forward reach of the hind leg equals the rear extension. The thrust of correct movement is seen when the rear pads are clearly exposed during rear extension. Feet must travel parallel to the line of motion with no tendency to swing out, cross

EYE
Very dark in color, not piercing.

NOSE
Preferably
black in
color.

COAT
Sleek, glistening,
and often
slightly wavy.
Too profuse a
coat masks type.
Long hair all
over the body is
a fault.

EAR
Hair longer on
ears, slightly
wavy.

FORECHEST
Furnished with longer
hair than rest of body.

FEET
Compact with well-arched toes.

over, or interfere with each other. Short, choppy movement, rolling or high stepping gait, close or overly wide coming or going are incorrect. The Dachshund must have agility, freedom of movement, and endurance to do the work for which he was developed.

Temperament—The Dachshund is clever, lively and courageous to the point of rashness, preserving in above and below ground work, with all the senses well-developed. Any display of shyness is a serious fault.

SPECIAL CHARACTERISTICS OF THE THREE COAT VARIETIES

The Dachshund is bred with three varieties of coat: (1) Smooth; (2) Wirehaired; (3) Longhaired, and is shown in two sizes, standard and miniature. All three varieties and both sizes must conform to the characteristics already specified. The following features are applicable for each variety:

Smooth Dachshund

Coat—Short, smooth and shining. Should be neither too long nor too thick. Ears not leathery. *Tail*—Gradually tapered to a point, well but not too richly haired. Long sleek bristles on the underside are considered a patch of strong-growing hair, not a fault. A brush tail is a fault, as is also a partly or wholly hairless tail.

Color of Hair—Although base color is immaterial, certain patterns and basic colors predominate. One-colored Dachshunds include red (with or without a shading of interspersed dark hairs or sable) and cream. A small amount of white on the chest

This black and tan smooth dam has produced a marvelous litter of black and tan pups, of course all smoothhaired.

Play and socialization are vital to the development of any dog. Give your young Dachsie safe playthings. Always supervise carefully with any toy that the dog can possibly destroy.

is acceptable, but not desirable. Nose and nails—black.

Two-colored Dachshunds include black, chocolate, wild boar, gray (blue) and fawn (Isabella), each with tan markings over the eyes, on the sides of the jaw and underlip, on the inner edge of the ear, front, breast, inside and behind the front legs, on the paws and around the anus, and from there to about one-third to one-half of the length of the tail on the underside. Undue prominence or extreme lightness of tan markings is undesirable. A small amount of white on the chest is acceptable but not desirable. Nose and nails—in the case of black dogs, black; for chocolate and for all other colors, dark brown, but self-colored is acceptable.

Dappled Dachshunds—The "single" dapple pattern is expressed as lighter colored areas contrasting with the darker base color, which may be any acceptable color. Neither the light nor the dark color should predominate. Nose and nails are the same as for one-and two-colored Dachshunds. Partial or wholly blue (wall) eyes are as acceptable as dark eyes. A large area of white on the chest of a dapple is permissible.

A "double" dapple is one in which varying amounts of white coloring occur over the body in addition to the dapple pattern. Nose and nails: as for one- and two-colored Dachshunds; partial or wholly self-colored is permissible. Brindle is a pattern (as opposed to a color) in which black or dark stripes occur over the entire body, although in some specimens the pattern may be visible only in the tan points.

Wirehaired Dachshund

Coat—With the exception of jaw, eyebrows, and ears, the whole body is covered with a uniform tight, short, thick, rough, hard, outer coat but with finer, somewhat softer, shorter hairs (undercoat) everywhere distributed between the coarser hairs. The absence of an undercoat is a fault. The distinctive facial furnishings include a beard and eyebrows. On the ears the hair is shorter than on the body, almost smooth. The general arrangement of the hair is such that the wirehaired Dachshund, when viewed from a distance, resembles the smooth. *Any sort of hair in the outer coat, wherever found on the body, especially on the top of the head, is a fault.* The same is true of long, curly, or wavy hair, or hair that sticks out irregularly in all directions. *Tail*—Robust, thickly haired, gradually tapering to a point. A flag tail is a fault. **Color of Hair**—While the most common colors are wild boar, black and tan, and various shades of red, all colors are admissible. A

Two handsome wirehaired Dachshunds in black and tan and red brindle. Brindle is a pattern as opposed to a color and refers to black or dark stripes occurring over the body.

Young wirehaired Dachsie puppies will develop a harder coat with age. Wirehaired puppies, however, are always unmistakably harsh coated and never smooth or silky.

small amount of white on the chest, although acceptable, is not desirable. Nose and nails—same as for the smooth variety.

Longhaired Dachshund

Coat—The sleek, glistening, often slightly wavy hair is longer under the neck and on the forechest, the underside of the body, the ears, and behind the legs. The coat gives the dog an elegant appearance. Short hair on the ear is not desirable. Too profuse a coat which masks type, equally long hair over the whole body, a curly coat, or a pronounced parting on the back are faults. **Tail**—Carried gracefully in prolongation of the spine; the hair attains its greatest length here and forms a veritable flag. **Color of Hair**—Same as for the smooth Dachshund. Nose and nails: same as for the smooth.

The foregoing description is that of the ideal Dachshund. Any deviation from the above described dog must be penalized to the extent of the deviation keeping in mind the importance of the contribution of the various features toward the basic original purpose of the breed.

Disqualification

Knuckling over of front legs.

The miniature Dachshund has been called both *Zwergteckel* and *Kaninchenteckel,* referring to first his size (*Zwerg* means dwarf) and second his ability to catch rabbits (*Kaninchen* means rabbit)!

THE MINIATURE DACHSHUND

Miniature Dachshunds are not under-sized or undeveloped specimens of full-sized Dachshunds but were purposely produced to work in burrows smaller than standard-sized Dachshunds could enter. The limits set upon their weight and chest circumference resulted in more slender body structure. Depth of chest and shortness of leg proportionate to standard conformation would, in these diminutive animals, prove impractical. "Within the American size limit of 'under nine pounds at twelve months or older,' symmetrical adherence to the general Dachshund conformation, combined with smallness, and mental and physical vitality, should be the outstanding characteristics of miniature Dachshunds." Written in 1935, describing the ideal miniature, these are the operative words for the application of the American standard to American miniature Dachshunds.

Miniatures like standards come in all three coat types: smooth, wire and long. They also come in a many colors and combinations of colors.

KANINCHENHUND

In the 1890s an attempt was made in Germany to quickly produce a dog with a chest girth under ten inches, small enough to dash freely through their acres of rabbit warrens to scare out the living prospective material for hassenpfeffer. Toy breeds used to shortcut the size-reduction also handed along toy temperament. These crash-dive, small-sized crossbred dogs would not hunt rabbits. The *Kaninchenhund* (rabbit dog) project collapsed, leaving behind a few spindling mixed-breed pets, some of whom resembled Dachshunds.

ZWERG AND KANINCHENTECKEL

Rabbits still abounded, free for the harvesting, so another approach was made—this time by experienced Dachshund breeders—to breed down in size from existing strains of *gebrauch teckel* (working, i.e., hunting Dachshunds) weighing around twelve pounds; this time, however, every individual retained in the size-reduction program was tested for "hunting passion" and any which did not prove true to type in this respect was discarded. By 1903 records disclose elaborate weight and chest circumference specifications (since World War II, German specifications no longer include weights, only

been trained to detect truffles! In Germany, puppies of Kaninchen sires and Zwerg dams are not classified until they are one year old. These slightly larger Zwergteckel incline toward better bone, substance, and type, more as sought in American Miniature Dachshund breeding.)

This utilitarian size-reduction

Zwergteckel don't hunt dwarfs—they *are* dwarfs! These two handsome dwarfs are too young to hunt rabbits.

chest-girth limits) and registrations of Zwerg (dwarf) teckel, and by 1918 of Kaninchen (rabbit) teckel, with chest-girth limits to enable these breeds to scurry freely through cottontail burrows. (A *Dachs*hund hunts badgers; a *kaninchen*teckel hunts rabbits, but a *zwerg*teckel does not hunt dwarfs—although some have

program sacrificed Dachshund appearance to functional qualities of ferret-slim body and zeal to hunt rabbits. Whatever abnormal glandular or other metabolic factors contributed to rapid size-reduction also evoked torsionally everted elbows and/ or forefeet, leggy proportions, prominent round eyes, smaller muzzles, abrupt stops, domed

Although Dachshunds today are rarely used to hunt, they should still possess the desire to do so. Most miniature Dachshunds today will chase a passing rabbit or squirrel in the back yard. This lovely harlequin Dachshund is primarily a pet and show dog.

skulls, and button ears—among the oldest breed faults, proving small size is no mutation. None of these faults handicap speed through rabbit holes, and they were anchored by impatient close breeding, in ever-smaller males—however little some of the smallest "nasturtium seed" studs resembled acceptable Dachshunds. Because females

"MINIATURES"

Zwerg and Kaninchenteckel were imported to the U.S. in the early 1930s as "cute" canine novelties. The name "miniature" Dachshund was adopted in place of the more complicated German nomenclature, or the American "toy"; the complex German specifications were rounded off simply to "under nine pounds;"

Minis are the favorite of small children. They are the perfect size for walking and playing and should not be classified as "toy" dogs.

carry and deliver puppies, they were spared extreme concentration of size reduction, and they better maintained their conformation. There seems probably some sex linkage with conformation, for to this day female miniatures were exhibited at dog shows; many conformation judges refused to "rate" them or judge them. Their field trials were scored by how many rabbits each contestant was able to bolt in ten minutes by stop watch.

and a combined-coat-and-sex class was offered for them at the May 6, 1934 Hotel Pennsylvania specialty show of the Dachshund Club of America with nine entries by four owners. That autumn several six- or seven-month-old puppies of standard parents won over miniature Dachshunds in this "under-nine-pound" class. To prevent such "ringers" from taking unfair advantage of this class, the minimum age of twelve months was added to the class definition

Call me elegant, call me dashing and sporting, but don't ever call me "cute"! The Dachshund resents being considered a "ladies' dog" and may not respond to soft cooing.

in 1935, and the Miniature Class was made a division of the Open Class, making blue-ribbon winners eligible to compete in Winners Classes with standard Dachshunds for championship points.

EARLY AMERICANA

In the U.S., it is doubtful if one Dachshund in a thousand is used

Our first miniature won the first weight-and-age Miniature Class at Westminster in 1935 and enough more that first year for the first "phantom" miniature championship. Her eight-pound size, good looks, and beguiling disposition helped favorably to introduce miniature Dachshunds in the East and Midwest. Another miniature that matured at four-

Dachshunds are prized in America, primarily as pets. Although many people spoil Dachshunds as they would a toy dog, no self-respecting Dachshund—even a puppy— would allow himself to be treated as a "lap dog."

to hunt game. Here the distinctive appeal of miniature Dachshunds as pets of diminutive and nimble, but well-balanced, unmistakable Dachshund type. In this scaling down process, clearance under the keel—already too low in many standard Dachshunds—cannot be reduced in proportion to other dimensions without curtailing their capacity to climb stairs, enter automobiles, or jump into your lap if invited.

and-a-quarter pounds, while less symmetrical in conformation, could go almost anywhere in a jacket pocket; she learned to relax under a napkin in restaurants where no one suspected her presence until she followed us out the door when we left. A six-pound miniature we took along on a rail and plane trip to California was permitted (in a shoulder-holster pouch) to sit at the dining car table for dinner, and the

Dachshund puppies are portable and lovable!

Pullman conductor beamed while she held court in the observation car. Hotels asked questions only if her crate appeared in the lobby. On only one of five planes that we flew did regulations require us to be separated.

EARLY PROBLEMS

In the first decade of miniature breeding in America, there were with too-rapid size reduction were concentrated. Whenever fairly close line-breeding was attempted to expedite a program, either improved quality brought with it increased size or reduced size or it entailed the same faults as in Germany: fiddle fronts, weedy structure, pop eyes, snipy muzzles, steep stops, apple domes, and bat ears.

Because miniature Dachshunds are designated by a weight differentiation, they are not granted separate status at dog shows according to A.K.C. policy. Three *more* Dachshund breeds would mean *six* Dachshunds competing in the Group ring.

so few miniatures, either imported from Germany or their immediate descendants—using the German gauge of three generations of unmixed miniature ancestry—that sound breeding plans were difficult to develop and harder still to carry out. All miniature stock had comparatively recent ancestors of standard size *and* ancestors in which faults linked

A.K.C. POSITION

These faults are among the reasons for the unwillingness of the A.K.C. to approve separate "variety" status for miniature Dachshunds; no breed variety is based upon weight limitation. There is not enough difference in height at shoulder to separate miniatures from standard Dachshunds. Miniature breeding

This handsome smooth Dachsie is a smart shopper! If your pet shop allows dogs inside, take your dog along for the ride. Of course, the educated Dachshund will pass the rawhide for a Nylabone® every time!

is not yet self-sustaining within their own size range. Separate miniature Winners Classes would entail complete miniature classification including Puppy Classes. And with three coat varieties established, separate varieties for the miniature size would complicate the classification by having an unprecedented result—six championship varieties in one breed!

POST-WAR IMPROVEMENT

Gradually increasing numbers of loyal devotees of miniature Dachshunds persisted in breeding and exhibiting them; and in the many years since World War II, they have enjoyed a renaissance of interest and favor. Patience and perseverance with slower, more selective approaches to producing miniatures in the image of good Dachshunds—ever reinforced and intensified by exactions of competition with standard Dachshunds—have achieved the double goal of a number of individuals of real championship quality in all three coats, accomplished well under the original nine-pound weight limit. The next objective is to engender a broader average of such high quality more dependably among more miniature Dachshunds.

A huddle of juvenile Dachshunds pondering post-war Dachshund history. None of these tots are ready for the Puppy Class.

PERSONALITY

DACHSHUND DISPOSITION

For centuries, Dachshunds have lived harmoniously with people. A Dachshund can share every family mood: exuberant when you are gay; rarin' to go when you are ready for a walk, a ride, or a boisterous game; happy to curl up near you when you are engaged in a settled occupation; and most responsive to every demonstration of your affection. It is a fallacy that all individuals of any one breed have this or that disposition. Temperaments vary; we have had Dachshunds that were "little pals of all the world," or preferring our family, sometimes one individual. We often can relate these choices to early environment. Each puppy inherits some degree of confident or shy temperament, and early associations often have lasting influences. Given a sound base, your regime can mold the finished

One of the world's little pals, this Dachshund pup will engage his new owners with his antics for many months to come.

product if you are firm, patient, and consistent.

NOT TO RUN FREE

Self-reliant character is just as deeply rooted in the Dachshund as its two-dogs-long-and-half-a-dog-high proportions, and it introduces a most serious problem! No family should acquire a Dachshund that expects it to run loose; it is never safe from the hazards of street or highway traffic. Let a Dachshund be inspired to cross the street, and no consideration of approaching automobiles will enter its head.

Part of the price of enjoying a Dachshund through the engaging humorous months of its unfolding puppyhood, through the long vigorous plateau of its adult life, into the mellow late years, is never—repeat *never*—to turn a Dachshund loose where it has access to traffic or traffic has access to it.

ABOVE: Well-trained children can spend many hours outdoors with a well-trained Dachshund. BELOW: Be sure your grounds are fenced in for the safety of your children and your Dachshund.

Handling young puppies is vital to their development as canine companions. Some puppies will require extra attention to bring them out of their shells; others are naturally expressive and explosive.

LEAVING YOUR PET ALONE

A dog is a gregarious animal. If your plan for living is such that a pet animal will be left alone as a daily routine, we recommend some other type of pet, although a *person* alone much of the time will find a world of comfort in a Dachshund's companionship. Don't make the mistake that one puppy provides good company for another puppy. Two puppies only become rivals for your attention—or they may revert to a canine community of their own, remote from people—and immensely complicate housebreaking and training. On the other hand, a Dachshund in its declining years may be stimulated by the presence of a puppy and, by its good example, can be of inestimable help in inducting a young successor to the ways of your household.

Clear eyes, a shiny coat, a moist nose—you can be pretty sure your Dachshund is feeling his best!

YOUR HEALTHY DACHSHUND

Your Dachshund is the image of good health: a glistening, clean coat, clear eyes, pink gums, moist nose, and ever-alert and active. We know our pets, their moods and habits, and therefore we can recognize when our Dachshund is experiencing an off-day. Signs of sickness can be very obvious or very subtle. As any mother can attest, diagnosing and treating an ailment requires common sense, knowing when to seek home remedies and when to visit your doctor, or veterinarian, as the case may be.

Your veterinarian, we know, is your Dachshund's best friend, next to you. It will pay to be choosy about your veterinarian. Talk to dog-owning friends whom you respect. Visit more than one vet before you make a lifelong choice. Trust your instincts. Find a knowledgeable, compassionate vet who knows Dachshunds and likes them.

Healthy young puppies should be alert and curious about their surroundings.

MAJOR HEALTH CONCERNS

Let's examine some of the problems that our breed can experience. Remember, despite the many problems to which Dachshunds may be prone, the breed has a life expectancy of 14 to 16 years, which is very promising for any dog!

Due to the Dachshund's unique back construction, the most prominent problem with which breeders concern themselves is intervertebral disk disease (IVD), which we might equate with slipped disk in humans. In the Dachshund, due to the stunted growth of the legs, IVD occurs in relatively young dogs, commonly as young as one year old. In other breeds affected, IVD occurs toward old age. Depending on the individual case, surgery or medical therapy is selected by the veterinarian and owner.

Owners are advised to keep their Dachshunds from jumping on furniture, climbing steep stairs, or any other strenuous

Initially the virus localizes in the dog's tonsils and then disperses to the liver, kidney and eyes. Generally speaking the dog's immune system is capable of combating this virus. Canine infectious hepatitis affects dogs whose systems cannot fight off the adenovirus. Affected dogs have fever, abdominal pains, bruising on mucous membranes and gums, and experience coma and convulsions. Prevention of hepatitis exists only through vaccination at eight to ten weeks of age and then boosters three or four weeks later, then annually.

Leptospirosis is a bacterium-related disease, often spread by rodents. The organisms that spread leptospirosis enter through the mucous membrane and spread to the internal organs via the bloodstream. It can be passed through the dog's urine. Leptospirosis does not affect young dogs as consistently as the other viruses; it is reportedly regional in distribution and somewhat dependent on the immunostatus of the dog. Fever, inappetence, vomiting, dehydration, hemorrhage, kidney and eye disease can result in moderate cases.

Bordetella, called canine cough, causes a persistent hacking cough in dogs and is very contagious. Bordetella involves a virus and a bacteria: parainfluenza is the most common virus implicated; *Bordetella bronchiseptica*, the bacterium. Bronchitis and pneumonia result in less than 20

Don't leave young puppies alone and unattended. Remember to puppy-proof every room to which your wandering Dachshunds will have access.

Dogs exposed to other dogs at dog shows require complete and up-to-date vaccinations. This Dachshund quintet is participating at the World Dog Show.

percent of the cases, and most dogs recover from the condition within a week to four weeks. Non-prescription medicines can help relieve the hacking cough, though nothing can cure the condition before it's run its course. Vaccination cannot guarantee protection from canine cough, but it does ward off the most common virus responsible for the condition.

Lyme disease (also called borreliosis), although known since for decades, was only first diagnosed in dogs in 1984. Lyme disease can affect cats, cattle, and horses, but especially people. In the U.S., the disease is transmitted by two ticks carrying the *Borrelia burgdorferi* organism: the deer tick (*Ixodes scapularis*) and the western

black-legged tick (*Ixodes pacificus*), the latter primarily affects reptiles. In Europe, *Ixodes ricinus* is responsible for spreading Lyme. The disease causes lameness, fever, joint swelling, inappetence, and lethargy. Removal of ticks from the dog's coat can help reduce the chances of Lyme, though not as much as avoiding heavily wooded areas where the dog is most likely to contract ticks. A vaccination is available, though has not been proven to protect dogs from all strains of the organism that cause the disease.

Rabies is passed to dogs and people through wildlife: in North America, principally through the skunk, fox and raccoon; the bat is not the culprit it was once thought to be. Likewise, the common image of the rabid dog foaming at the mouth with every hair on end is unlikely the truest scenario. A rabid dog exhibits difficulty eating, salivates much and has spells of paralysis and awkwardness. Before a dog reaches this final state, it may

COPING WITH PARASITES

Parasites have clung to our pets for centuries. Despite our modern efforts, fleas still pester our pet's existence, and our own. All dogs itch, and fleas can make even the happiest dog a miserable, scabby mess. The loss of hair and habitual biting and chewing at

Dachshunds who lead indoor/outdoor lives will inevitably contract fleas at some point. In order to control flea problems, the dog as well as the whole indoor environment must be thoroughly treated.

experience anxiety, personality changes, irritability and more aggressiveness than is usual. Vaccinations are strongly recommended as affected dogs are too dangerous to manage and are commonly euthanized. Puppies are generally vaccinated at 12 weeks of age, and then annually. Although rabies is on the decline in the world community, tens of thousands of humans die each year from rabies-related incidents.

themselves rank among the annoyances; the nuisances include the passing of tapeworms and the whole family itching through the summer months. A full range of flea-control and elimination products are available at pet shops, and your veterinarian surely has recommendations. Sprays, powders, collars and dips fight fleas from the outside; drops and pills fight the good fight from inside. Discuss the possibilities with your vet. Not all products can be used in conjunction with one another, and some dogs may be more sensitive to certain applications than others. The dog's living quarters must be debugged as well as the dog itself. Heavy infestation may require multiple treatments.

Always check your dog for ticks well. Although fleas can be acquired almost anywhere, ticks are more likely to be picked up in heavily treed areas, pastures or other outside grounds (such as dog shows or obedience or field trials). Athletic, active, and hunting dogs are the most likely subjects, though any passing dog can be the host. Remember Lyme disease is passed by tick infestation.

As for internal parasites, worms are potentially dangerous for dogs and people. Roundworms, hookworms, whipworms, tapeworms, and heartworms comprise the blightsome party of troublemakers. Deworming puppies begins at around two to three weeks and continues until three months of age. Proper hygienic care of the environment is also important to prevent contamination with roundworm and hookworm eggs. Heartworm preventatives are recommended by most veterinarians, although there are some drawbacks to the regular introduction of poisons into our dogs' system. These daily or monthly preparations also help regulate most other worms as well. Discuss worming procedures with your veterinarian.

Roundworms pose a great threat to dogs and people. They are found in the intestines of dogs, and can be passed to

All puppies will need to be immunated on time and to receive necessary wormings. Your veterinarian will provide an appropriate schedule.

people through ingestion of feces-contaminated dirt. Roundworm infection can be prevented by not walking dogs in heavy-traffic people areas, by burning feces, and by curbing dogs in a responsible manner. (Of course, in most areas of the country, curbing dogs is the law.) Roundworms are typically passed from the bitch to the litter, and bitches should be treated along with the puppies, even if she tested negative prior to whelping. Generally puppies are treated every two weeks until two months of age.

Hookworms, like roundworms, are also a danger to dogs and people. The hookworm parasite (known as *Ancylostoma caninum*) causes cutaneous larva migrans in people. The eggs of hookworms are passed in feces and become infective in shady, sandy areas. The larvae penetrate the skin of the dog, and the dog subsequently becomes infected. When swallowed, these parasites affect the intestines, lungs, windpipe, and the whole digestive system. Infected dogs suffer from anemia and lose large amounts of blood in the places where the worms latch onto the dog's intestines, etc.

Although infrequently passed to humans, whipworms are cited as one of the most common parasites

The great outdoors can be dangerous to your Dachshund. Fleas and ticks can be picked up by your dog, so check him over carefully as soon as he comes back indoors.

in America. These elongated worms affect the intestines of the dog, where they latch on, and cause colic upset or diarrhea. Unless identified in stools passed, whipworms are difficult to diagnose. Adult worms can be eliminated more consistently than the larvae, since whipworms live unusual life cycles. Proper hygienic care of outdoor grounds is critical to the avoidance of these harmful parasites.

Tapeworms are carried by fleas, and enter the dog when the dog swallows the flea. Humans can acquire tapeworms in the same way, though we are less likely to swallow fleas than dogs are. Recent studies have shown that certain rodents and other wild animals have been infected with tapeworms, and dogs can be affected by catching and/or eating these other animals. Of course, outdoor hunting dogs and terriers are more likely to be infected in this way than are your typical house dog or non-motivated hound. Treatment for tapeworm has proven very effective, and infected dogs do not show great discomfort or symptoms. When people are infected, however, the liver can be seriously damaged. Proper cleanliness is the best bet against tapeworms.

Heart-worm disease is transmitted by mosquitoes and badly affects the lungs, heart and blood vessels of dogs. The larvae of *Dirofilaria immitis* enter the dog's bloodstream when bitten by an infected mosquito. The

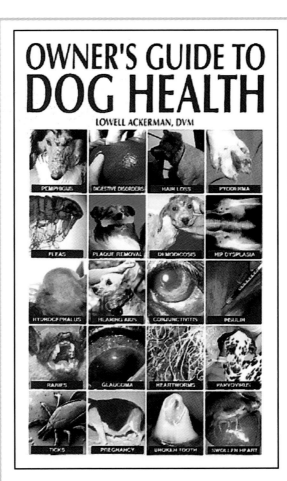

Owner's Guide to Dog Health by Dr. Lowell Ackerman is the undisputed champion of dog health books. This encyclopedic volume covers every subject that any dog owner might need. It actually is a complete veterinarian's handbook in simple, easy-to-understand language.

In order to isolate a dog from the rest of the house, consider using baby gates in the doorway. This is a cost-effective, efficient way to confine a dog from children or other animals.

Littermates commonly eat out of the same feeding containers. If one member of the litter picks up a parasite, generally the entire litter is affected. For adult dogs, it is best to feed each animal in a separate bowl.

larvae take about six months to mature. Infected dogs suffer from weight loss, appetite loss, chronic coughing and general fatigue. Not all affected dogs show signs of illness right away, and carrier dogs may be affected for years before clinical signs appear. Treatment of heartworm disease has been effective but can be dangerous also. Prevention as always is the desirable alternative. Ivermectin is the active ingredient in most heartworm preventatives and has proven to be successful. Check with your veterinarian for the preparation best for your dog. Dogs generally begin taking the preventatives at eight months of age, and continue to do so throughout the non-winter months.

Although an old wives' tale says candy will give your dog worms, it is true that it will upset his digestion.

DACHSHUND'S DENTAL HEALTH

Puppies and young Dachshunds need something with resistance to chew on while their teeth and jaws are developing—for cutting the puppy teeth, to induce growth of the permanent teeth under the puppy teeth, to assist in getting rid of the puppy teeth at the proper time, to help the permanent teeth through the gums, to ensure normal jaw development, and to settle the permanent teeth solidly in the jaws.

The adult Dachshund's desire to chew stems from the instinct for tooth cleaning, gum massage, and jaw exercise—plus the need for an outlet for periodic doggie tensions.

This is why dogs, especially puppies and young dogs, will often destroy property worth hundreds of dollars when their chewing instinct is not diverted from their owner's possessions. And this is why you should provide your Dachshund with

something to chew—something that has the necessary functional qualities, is desirable from the Dachshund's viewpoint, and is safe for him.

It is very important that your Dachshund not be permitted to chew on anything he can break or on any indigestible thing from which he can bite sizable chunks. Sharp pieces, such as

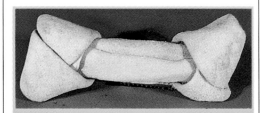

Rawhide is probably the most popular dog chew. It can be dangerous and cause a dog to choke on it, as it swells when wet.

from a bone which can be broken by a dog, may pierce the intestinal wall and kill. Indigestible things that can be bitten off in chunks, such as from shoes or rubber or plastic toys, may cause an intestinal stoppage (if not regurgitated) and bring painful death, unless surgery is promptly performed.

Strong natural bones, such as 4- to 8-inch lengths of round shin bone from mature beef—either the kind you can get from a butcher or one of the variety available commercially in pet stores—may serve your Dachshund's teething needs if

Pet shops sell real bones that have been colored, cooked, dyed or served natural. Some of the bones are huge but still can be destroyed by a Dachshund.

his mouth is large enough to handle them effectively. You may be tempted to give your Dachshund puppy a smaller bone and he may not be able to break it when you do, but puppies grow rapidly and the power of their jaws constantly increases until maturity. This means that a growing Dachshund may break one of the smaller bones at any time, swallow the pieces, and die painfully before you realize what is wrong.

All hard natural bones are very abrasive. If your Dachshund is an avid chewer, natural bones may wear away his teeth prematurely; hence, they then should be taken away from your dog when the teething purposes have been served. The badly worn, and usually painful, teeth of many mature dogs can be traced to excessive chewing on natural bones.

Contrary to popular belief, knuckle bones that can be chewed up and swallowed by your Dachshund provide little, if any, usable calcium or other nutriment. They do, however, disturb the digestion of most dogs and cause them to vomit the nourishing food they need.

Dried rawhide products of various types, shapes, sizes, and prices are available on the market and have become quite popular. However, they don't serve the primary chewing functions very well; they are a bit messy when wet from mouthing, and most Dachshunds chew them up rather rapidly—but they have been considered safe for dogs until recently. Now, more and more incidents of death, and near death, by strangulation have been reported to be the results of partially swallowed

The Nylabone/Gumabone Pooch Pacifiers enable the dog to slowly chew off the knobs while they clean their own teeth. These pacifiers are very effective as detailed scientific studies have proven.

chunks of rawhide swelling in the throat. More recently, some veterinarians have been attributing cases of acute constipation to large pieces of incompletely digested rawhide in the intestine.

A new product, molded rawhide, is very safe. During the process, the rawhide is melted and then injection molded into the familiar dog shape. It is very hard and is eagerly accepted by Dachshunds. The melting process also sterilizes the rawhide. Don't confuse this with pressed rawhide, which is nothing more than small strips of rawhide squeezed together.

The nylon bones, especially those with natural meat and bone fractions added, are probably the most complete, safe, and economical answer to the chewing need. Dogs cannot break them or bite off sizable chunks; hence, they are completely safe—and being longer lasting than other things offered for the purpose, they are economical.

Hard chewing raises little bristle-like projections on the surface of the nylon bones—to provide effective interim tooth cleaning and vigorous gum massage, much in the same way your toothbrush does it for you. The little projections are raked off and swallowed in the form of thin shavings, but the chemistry of the nylon is such that they break down in the stomach fluids and pass through without effect.

The toughness of the nylon provides the strong chewing resistance needed for important jaw exercise and effectively aids teething functions, but there is no tooth wear because nylon is non-abrasive. Being inert, nylon does not support the growth of microorganisms; and it can be washed in soap and water or it can be sterilized by boiling or in an autoclave.

Nylabone® is highly recommended by veterinarians as a safe, healthy nylon bone that can't splinter or chip. Nylabone® is frizzled by the dog's chewing action, creating a toothbrush-like surface that cleanses the teeth and massages the gums. Nylabone®, the only chew products made of flavor-impregnated solid nylon, are available in your local pet shop. Nylabone® is superior to the cheaper bones because it is made of virgin nylon, which is the strongest and longest-lasting type of nylon available. The cheaper bones are made from recycled or re-ground nylon scraps, and have a tendency to break apart and split easily.

Nothing, however, substitutes for periodic professional attention for your Dachshund's teeth and gums, not any more than your toothbrush can do that for you. Have your Dachshund's teeth cleaned at least once a year by your veterinarian (twice a year is better) and he will be happier, healthier, and far more pleasant to live with.